W9-BMA-544

RELIGION IN THE ROMAN EMPIRE

BEN HOLTZER

Cavendish Square

New York

Published in 2017 by Cavendish Square Publishing, LLC
243 5th Avenue, Suite 136, New York, NY 10016

Copyright © 2017 by Cavendish Square Publishing, LLC

First Edition

No part of this publication may be reproduced, stored in a retrieval system, or transmitted in any form or by any means—electronic, mechanical, photocopying, recording, or otherwise—without the prior permission of the copyright owner. Request for permission should be addressed to Permissions, Cavendish Square Publishing, 243 5th Avenue, Suite 136, New York, NY 10016. Tel (877) 980-4450; fax (877) 980-4454.

Website: cavendishsq.com

This publication represents the opinions and views of the author based on his or her personal experience, knowledge, and research. The information in this book serves as a general guide only. The author and publisher have used their best efforts in preparing this book and disclaim liability rising directly or indirectly from the use and application of this book.

CPSIA Compliance Information: Batch #CW17CSQ

All websites were available and accurate when this book was sent to press.

Library of Congress Cataloging-in-Publication Data

Names: Holtzer, Ben, author.
Title: Religion in the Roman Empire / Ben Holtzer.
Description: New York : Cavendish Square Publishing, 2017. | Series: Life in the Roman Empire | Includes bibliographical references and index.
Identifiers: LCCN 2016028950 (print) | LCCN 2016033562 (ebook) | ISBN 9781502622631 (library bound) | ISBN 9781502622648 (E-book)
Subjects: LCSH: Rome--Religion. | Rome--Religious life and customs.
Classification: LCC BL803 .H65 2017 (print) | LCC BL803 (ebook) | DDC 292.07--dc23
LC record available at https://lccn.loc.gov/2016028950

Editorial Director: David McNamara
Editor: Caitlyn Miller
Copy Editor: Nathan Heidelberger
Associate Art Director: Amy Greenan
Designer: Joseph Macri
Production Coordinator: Karol Szymczuk
Photo Research: J8 Media

The photographs in this book are used by permission and through the courtesy of: Cover Brian Jannsen/Alamy Stock Photo; p. 4 Werner Forman Archive/Heritage Images/Getty Images; p. 6 TTstudio/Shutterstock.com; p. 8 SF photo/Shutterstock.com; p. 10 DEA/A. DAGLI ORTI/De Agostini/Getty Images; p. 12 Yakov Oskano/Shutterstock.com; p. 16 Museo Archeologico Nazionale, Naples, Italy/Bridgeman Images; p. 19 soulofbeach/Shutterstock.com; p. 21 Edward Dodwell/File:Curse tablet made of lead - Dodwell Edward -1819.jpg/Wikimedia Commons; p. 24 Heinrich Kiepert/File:Heinrich Kiepert. Roma urbs ab Augusti Imp. tempore cum muris ab Aureliano et Honorio.jpg/Wikimedia Commons; p. 27 Leonid Andronov/Shutterstock.com; p. 29 sislavio/Shutterstock.com; p. 32 DeAgostini/Getty Images; p. 34 DEA/G. DAGLI ORTI/De Agostini/Getty Images; p. 39 Private Collection/The Stapleton Collection/Bridgeman Images; p. 40 Musee des Beaux-Arts, Lille, France/Bridgeman Images; p. 43 Nostell Priory, Yorkshire, UK/National Trust Photographic Library/Bridgeman Images; p. 45 ©Tarker/Bridgeman Images; p. 48 Alvaro German Vilela/Shutterstock.com; p. 54 Manchester Art Gallery, UK/Bridgeman Images; p. 57 Archives Charmet/Bridgeman Images; p. 59 Universal History Archive/Getty Images; p. 62 Hulton Archive/Getty Images; p. 69 National Gallery of Art, Washington DC, USA/Bridgeman Images.

Printed in the United States of America

Contents

THE HISTORY OF THE ROMAN EMPIRE

Mars was one of the most important gods in the ancient Roman belief system.

According to the ancient Romans, their empire began with a single city. They claimed that this city, Rome, was founded by a man who was reared for a time by a wolf. In their creation myth, Romulus and Remus were the twin sons of a priestess (who was also the daughter of King Numitor) and Mars, the god of war. Numitor's brother Amulius held the throne at the time of the twins' birth. Amulius felt that Romulus and Remus were a threat to his power, so he decided to have them killed. Yet the twins survived the attempt on their lives and traveled down the Tiber River to a new region, where a wolf (and a woodpecker) provided them with sustenance until a local man took them in. Romulus would ultimately kill Remus and name the city they founded after himself.

This legendary start to the empire provides a lot of information about the customs and spiritual beliefs of the ancient Romans. Priests, priestesses, gods, goddesses, and poets all played central roles in Romans' everyday lives. And though they held fast to their myths, in reality Rome was founded in 753 BCE by fisherman and farmers. Historians know little about the earliest days of the empire, but we do know that Romans spent the so-called regal period conquering territories throughout modern-day Italy. During this period, Rome was ruled by kings. In 509 BCE, Rome became a republic, and its rulers were elected. The republic lasted only until 27 BCE, when the first emperor took power. The Roman Empire would be ruled by emperors until its collapse.

Religion was extremely important to the Roman state and to the Romans' sense of themselves. In this book, you'll meet religious figures and everyday worshippers. Understanding the religious beliefs of ancient Rome is critical to understanding life in the Roman Empire.

Chapter One

The Divine
and the
Human

The Pantheon, a temple built to honor all of the gods, still stands in the city of Rome.

"If we compare our history to that of other nations, we shall see that although we may be equal or inferior to them in other respects, we outshine them by far in religion, that is to say, in the worship of the gods."

—Cicero

Many of the Romans' religious beliefs trace back to the Greeks and the Etruscans. Roman gods and goddesses are, in fact, a mixture of new inventions and existing deities from conquered cultures. Scholars suggest that the Romans felt uncertain about which gods were the "correct" gods and therefore worshipped as many as possible in an attempt to gain favor. As the Roman Empire grew, there were more gods to choose from. The **pantheon** of gods did not always increase with new conquests, though. Any god or goddess that served a similar role to an existing Roman god was merely combined with the one the ancient Romans already worshipped.

The Roman belief system included gods and goddesses who correlated to specific interests (like health or love), personal gods worshipped at home, and the concept of unifying spiritual forces called numina.

Numina

The Romans, like many peoples, felt that there was a kind of divine force or spirit present in every activity, in everything in the natural world, and even in the objects of daily life. This spirit was often called a numen (the plural form is numina). Awareness of the numina gave pious Romans the sense that the divine took part in all they did, wherever they went. For example, when they entered or left their homes, they were interacting with the numen of the threshold, Limentinus; when they swept the floor, the numen Deverra was present in the broom. A farmer tending his grain crop saw the powers of many numina at work, including Seia, the guardian of the seed while it was underground; Segetia, the spirit of the ripening grain above ground; and Messor, the numen of harvesting.

The Tiber River

Abstract ideas, too, had their numina. These were often personified as deities, usually goddesses, such as Fortuna (Luck), Pax (Peace), and Victoria (Victory). Similarly, the numina of **provinces** and cities were portrayed and honored as goddesses: for example, Britannia (Britain) and Roma (Rome). River spirits might be thought of as male or female: the Tiber River in Italy was watched over by the god Tiberinus, while the goddess Sequana was the **personification** of the Seine River in what is now France. As these examples show, there might not be a clear-cut difference between numina and deities. In general, we can say that all deities were numina—divine powers—but many numina were not imagined to take on human characteristics as gods or goddesses.

Protective Spirits

Every individual also had a numen or guardian spirit. This was known as a *genius* for a man and a *iuno* for a woman. The Genius Paterfamilias was the spirit of the father of the family, the head of the household. It was often symbolized as a snake. This genius protected not only the father but also everyone else in the household, for whom the father was responsible.

Associated with the Genius Paterfamilias was the Lar, another kind of household guardian. Every family had its own particular Lar; some scholars think that the Lares (LAH-rays) were related to spirits of the family's ancestors.

In artwork, Lares were often portrayed as dancing young men. They were so closely linked to the home that a Roman expression for "returning home" was *redire ad Larem suum*: "to go back to one's Lar." Along with the Lares, Roman families honored their household's Penates (pe-NAH-tays), guardians of the pantry or food cupboard. There were also public Penates, whose worship was related to the well-being of Rome, as well as Lares who were honored at crossroads in every district of the city.

This bronze Lar dates to the second century BCE.

The hearth fire of each home was under the guardianship of the goddess Vesta, who was generally worshipped alongside the family Lares and Penates. Proper worship of Vesta was considered essential to the well-being of Rome. In her temple in the **Forum**, the heart of the city, the goddess was symbolized by an eternal flame, which was tended by a group of priestesses called the vestal virgins.

MAJOR GODS AND GODDESSES

While the Lares, Penates, and many numina had very specific areas of concern, the major deities looked after a wide range of interests. They were also felt to be particularly involved with the well-being of Rome and its empire. For this reason, they are often called "the gods of the state religion." This was the official, formal religion of the empire and was full of time-honored traditions that maintained the relationship between the Romans and their gods.

Chief among the deities was Jupiter, known as "the Best and Greatest." He was the chief protector of Rome, the giver of victory, and the guardian of emperors. In addition, like his Greek counterpart, Zeus, he was a god of the sky and the weather, especially thunderstorms. He also watched over agreements, contracts, and promises. Jupiter was often symbolized by an eagle.

Juno was the wife of Jupiter. She was particularly connected with women and marriage, but had other concerns as well. Like many Roman deities, she had a number of titles, which came from the various roles she played. Often she was called Juno Regina, "Juno the Queen." As Juno Lucina she was a goddess of light and of childbirth. She also had a military aspect and could be approached as Juno Curitis, "Juno of the Spear." Juno Sospita meant "Juno the Savior," referring to her role as a protector. Juno was closely identified with the Greek goddess Hera.

Minerva was mainly a goddess of crafts and warfare. As Minerva Medica, she was concerned with doctors and healing. In art she was generally shown wearing a helmet and might be holding a spear and shield, as was the corresponding Greek goddess, Athena.

Mars, often equated with the Greek Ares, is most familiar to us today as the Roman god of war. In the ancient world, however, he was also a protector of the crops and a god of springtime, when seeds were planted—this is why the month of March was named after him. Wolves and woodpeckers were sacred to Mars.

Venus, too, played various roles. We know her best as the goddess of love and beauty, like her Greek counterpart, Aphrodite. But Venus was also the numen of gardens, making them fertile to produce vegetables, fruit, and flowers. The Romans honored her as their divine ancestress, for she was the mother of Aeneas. This legendary hero, a refugee from the Trojan War, settled in Italy near the future site of Rome, and his descendant, Romulus, was said to have founded the city.

Mercurius, or Mercury, was the messenger of the gods. He was also a deity of abundance, trade, and success in business. Artists often portrayed Mercury in the same way as the Greek god Hermes, wearing winged shoes and a winged hat, carrying a staff with two snakes entwined around it (called a caduceus).

Other major Roman deities included Ceres, goddess of grain (equivalent to Greece's Demeter); Diana (Artemis), goddess of women, wild nature, hunting, and the moon; Apollo (whose name was the same in Greek), god of healing,

Commemorated here in a monumental sculpture, Jupiter was the most important Roman god.

prophecy, poetry, music, and the sun; Neptune (Poseidon), god of the sea and of horses; Hercules (Heracles), god of victory, strength, and business deals; Volcanus or Vulcan (Hephaestus to the Greeks), god of fire and metalworking; Pomona, goddess of fruit; Vertumnus, god of orchards and the changing seasons; Silvanus, a god of woodlands; and Castor, a god of horses, horsemen, athletes, and sailors. As can be seen, most of the deities of the state religion were felt to be quite similar to gods and goddesses from Greece. In fact, people in the eastern part of the empire usually worshipped the deities under their Greek names.

HOLY RULERS

Many peoples of the ancient Mediterranean world, including the Romans, did not draw a sharp line between the human and the divine. They recognized certain qualities as being godlike, and it was fairly easy to believe that people with those qualities could in fact become gods. The abilities to command armies, to win victories, to make laws, to govern peoples—these were all seen as having a kind of divine nature. It is not surprising, then, that the emperors, who wielded such powers, received divine honors.

The emperor Augustus was the adopted son of Julius Caesar, who was regarded as a god after his death. This made Augustus the son of a god, which increased his own authority. In some eastern provinces of the empire, where rulers had always been considered at least semidivine, Augustus and his successors were honored as gods not only after their deaths, but during their lifetimes as well. In Rome itself, however, Augustus refused to be worshipped. Instead, he encouraged people to honor his genius. Worshipping the emperor's guardian spirit quickly became an established and expected part of the state religion.

After Augustus died, he, like Julius Caesar, was officially deified (made a god)—as with Caesar, his achievements seemed superhuman. This was not the case with some of the succeeding emperors. In fact, the empire's third and fifth rulers, Gaius Caligula and Nero, were both egomaniacs who sought to be worshipped in Rome as gods during their lifetimes—for this and other reasons, both were hated by much of the Roman populace. The fourth emperor, Claudius, did better. He was deified after his death, for he had conquered Britain (something that even Caesar had not managed to do). By the last quarter of the first century CE, it was expected that all but the worst emperors would join the ranks of the gods after death.

A Savior for Every Circumstance

In addition to worshipping the great gods who ensured the well-being of the Roman people as a whole, individuals were often drawn to goddesses and gods who offered a more personal relationship. Many people were devoted to Aesculapius (in Greek, Asklepios), a god of healing. Worshippers in poor health might spend a night, or several nights, in his temple in the hope of receiving healing dreams from the god. These dreams could bring comfort, if nothing else. The **orator** and teacher Aelius Aristides had such an experience in a temple of Aesculapius in 146 CE. He described the transcendent feeling of the encounter in his writing.

Throughout the empire, the Egyptian goddess Isis inspired intense devotion. Many of her worshippers believed that all other goddesses were Isis under different names, playing different roles. Even under her own name, she was concerned with a great many things, among them love, childbirth, motherhood, healing, agriculture, weather, navigation, language, law, justice, war, and peace. Isis was a compassionate, merciful goddess who cared about the lives of those who prayed to her. Moreover, she could overrule the decrees of fate. She had restored her murdered husband, Osiris, to life, and so she also assured her followers a blessed afterlife.

Another deity who promised life after death was the god Bacchus. On one level, he was simply the god of wine, but in addition, he represented freedom and ecstasy. He was identified with grapevines, which die in winter and then come to life again in the spring. Cybele, or Magna Mater (meaning "The Great Mother"); Mithras, a god of light and truth; and the Greek earth goddesses Demeter and Persephone were also major deities who offered eternal life and the salvation or care of an individual's soul.

Pax Deorum

Religion was extremely important to the Roman state and to the Romans' sense of themselves. A centerpiece of Roman belief was the concept of *pax deorum*, "the peace of the gods"—the state of harmony and order that came with the proper relationship between humans and the deities. As long as the Roman people did their part to maintain pax deorum, it was believed, they and their empire would thrive. Gods and humans, after all, were members of the same community.

Polybius on the Role of Religion

Polybius was born in 200 BCE in Greece. After the Romans conquered his hometown in 168 BCE, he was sent to the city of Rome as a political prisoner. After working as a tutor for several years, he began writing a comprehensive history of the empire. This multivolume book took more than seven decades to write. Polybius's *Historiae* (*Histories*) is considered to be a valuable primary source because Polybius was an outsider who tried to write without bias. Polybius verified sources carefully and felt that there was no room for personal judgment in historical accounts, though he did occasionally offer opinions about Roman culture. For instance, Polybius had this to say about religion in ancient Rome:

> In my opinion, the area in which the Roman constitution is most conspicuously superior is their concept of the gods. It seems to me that the very thing that is a matter of reproach among other peoples is what holds the Roman state together: I mean *deisidaimonia*. Religious matters are dramatized and introduced into their public and private life to such an extent that nothing could exceed them in importance.

The term "deisidaimonia" translates roughly to "obedience to the gods." Polybius believed that religion could be useful politically. In his mind, obedience to the gods correlated with obedience to the emperor.

CHAPTER TWO

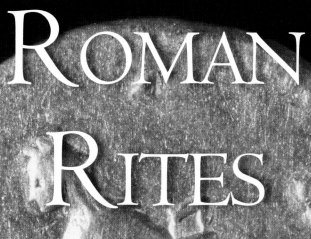

ROMAN RITES

This coin demonstrates the concept of *pietas* through its depiction of sacrifice; the word "pietas" also appears around its edge.

*"There is no place in our city that is not filled
with a sense of religion and the gods."*

—Livy

Worship in the ancient world could be as simple as a spoken
prayer to a god or goddess or as complex as a multistep
ritual. Many rituals required more than words: sacrifices
played a large role in many Roman rites. When we think
of sacrifices today, we often imagine gruesome scenes. Though so-called blood
sacrifice had a place in ancient Roman ritual, most sacrifices were innocuous.

Religion and daily life were intertwined, and both were guided by the
concept of *pietas*. The Romans understood this word to mean a proper sense
of duty that encompassed all areas of life. Pietas involved conscientiously
upholding correct, respectful relations with parents and other family members,
ancestors, fellow citizens, government authorities—and deities. A person with
pietas was careful to honor the gods by performing the traditional prayers
and ceremonies of the state religion. These had clearly pleased the gods in the
past, as the empire's strength proved, and so the established observances would
continue to win divine favor for the Romans.

Sacrifices and Prayers

The central part of most Roman religious rites was sacrifice. This was, literally, a sacred action, which involved making an offering to the gods. Because the deities gave so much to humans, it was considered only proper to give something back to them. The offerings could be fruit, flowers, wheat cakes or crackers, milk, wine, honey, or burning incense. They were often made on an altar before a statue of a goddess or god.

Major ceremonies generally called for blood sacrifice, which would take place at an outdoor altar. Although this practice may be difficult to understand today, it was common in ancient times. In the Roman Empire, an animal would be chosen depending on the ceremony's purpose and the deity being honored. For example, a cow would be sacrificed to Juno, but a bull to Mars. The animal had to be perfect in health and appearance, and it could not struggle as it was led to the altar—an obviously unwilling victim was unacceptable to the gods. At the altar, a priest burned incense and made a libation, or liquid offering, of wine. Then he **consecrated** the animal by sprinkling it with ground and salted grain (called *mola salsa*), pouring wine onto its head, and passing a knife over its back. An assistant then killed the animal; this was done swiftly, with as little pain as possible. Sometimes the whole body was dedicated to the deity and burned on the altar, but usually only certain parts were burned. The rest of the animal either provided meat for a feast among the priests and worshippers or was taken to be sold in the marketplace.

Sacrifices were always accompanied by prayers. These had to take a specific form and were very carefully worded. Prayers could also take the form of vows, in which the worshipper asked the deity to do something and promised to do something in return—usually to perform a sacrifice or set up an altar or statue

The altar, podium, and cella of the Temple of Vespasian in Pompeii

to the goddess or god in question. Poorer people might give a small plaque or clay figurine to a temple in fulfillment of a vow.

SIGNS FROM ABOVE

When Romans made a blood sacrifice, they generally wanted some sign that the deity had accepted the sacrifice and looked favorably on the worshipper. For this reason, men known as haruspices were called on to examine the animal's internal organs. A haruspex knew the normal shape, color, and condition of the organs. If there were deformities or other differences from what was normal, the haruspex understood what these symbolized. The Romans believed that the gods "imprinted" the marks of their favor or disfavor on the organs as the animal was being consecrated. If the signs showed that the sacrifice was unacceptable, a further sacrifice would have to be made.

Before a person took any major action, it was important to find out if the gods approved. This was another occasion when a haruspex might be called on to examine the organs of a sacrificed animal. In this case, if the signs were unfavorable, the person could abandon the project, wait until the signs were better, find some way to earn the gods' favor—or go ahead as planned and risk divine displeasure. But most Romans knew plenty of stories about what could happen to people who took these risks, such as generals who ignored the gods' warnings and suffered dreadful defeats.

Another way of learning whether the gods approved of an action or not was augury. This was also known as "taking the **auspices**." Augury generally involved marking out a particular area, in the sky or on the ground, and then watching and interpreting the behavior of birds in that area, especially eagles, vultures, and crows or ravens. The priests who explained what the birds' flight patterns and eating habits meant were called **augurs**. They were also

Hexes

In another kind of prayer (which scholars sometimes call a curse or hex), a person called on a deity to take action against a thief or other enemy. These prayers were often inscribed on sheets of lead and left in the temple of the god who was being appealed to.

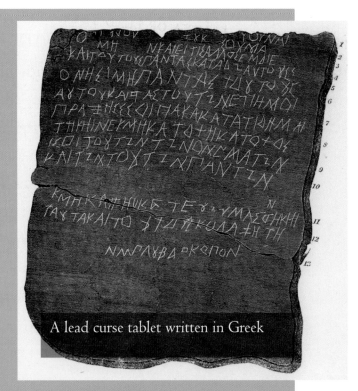

A lead curse tablet written in Greek

One example from southern Britain reads, "A memorandum to the god Mercury … from Saturnina a woman concerning the linen cloth she has lost. Let him who stole it not have rest before/unless/until he brings the aforesaid things to the temple, whether he is man or woman, slave or free."

Another example of a hex demonstrates the fervor of chariot racers and fans:

I call on you, demon, whoever you are, and ask that from this hour, from this day, from this moment, you torture and kill the horses of the Green and White teams, and that you kill and crush the drivers Clarus, Felix, Primulus, and Romanus, and that you leave not a breath in their bodies.

This hex was unearthed at a racetrack, demonstrating the importance of both the words of the hex and the location of the "curse tablet."

responsible for marking out various kinds of sacred boundaries, such as the places where temples would be built.

The deities could send warnings without being asked for them—sometimes through bolts of lightning, at other times through "prodigies." In general, prodigies were unusual happenings in the natural world, or they involved something being very out of place, such as a wild animal showing up within a city. Haruspices explained the meaning of lightning flashes and prodigies and recommended the proper actions to take in order to prevent the harm that was warned against. For example, when a horned owl—considered a very unlucky bird—was found in a temple in Rome in 43 CE, the whole city had to be purified and protected with sacrifices, prayers, and a solemn procession around the pomerium, or sacred boundary line.

THE MYSTERIES

For a great many Romans, this world was the only one with which they concerned themselves. They either did not believe in an afterlife or did not worry themselves about it. Residents of the empire who were drawn to the worship of deities such as Isis and Bacchus, on the other hand, were a good deal more interested in the world beyond this one. These worshippers did not reject the state religion, but alongside it they wanted a spiritual path that had a greater mystical, emotional, and personal feeling.

These "in-depth" spiritual practices have come to be known as the Mysteries, or mystery religions. The term comes from the Greek word *mystes*, "an initiate." Initiates were people who went through a ceremony that brought them closer to a particular goddess or god, deepened their understanding of the spiritual dimension of life, and gave them a promise of overcoming death. The ceremonies were kept secret from outsiders, and in any case were difficult to describe in words. These experiences were highly symbolic, and only someone who had been through them would really understand the meaning of them. In general, however, we can tell that initiations usually included purification, spiritual ordeals or trials, beholding sacred symbols, hearing sacred chants or stories about the deity, and a symbolic death and rebirth. This is how the second-century-CE orator and novelist Apuleius described initiation into the Mysteries of Isis:

> I approached the confines of death. I trod the threshold of Proserpine [the goddess of the Underworld]; and borne through the elements I returned. At midnight I saw the Sun shining in all his glory. I approached the gods below and the gods above, and I stood beside them, and I worshipped them. Behold, I have told my experience, and yet what you hear can mean nothing to you.

Like today, religion in Rome was deeply personal. Each person in ancient Rome viewed religion through a unique lens. Depending on social class, geographic location, and inclination to spirituality, a person might have placed their religion at the center of their life—like the initiates described above—or barely considered the gods and goddesses at all.

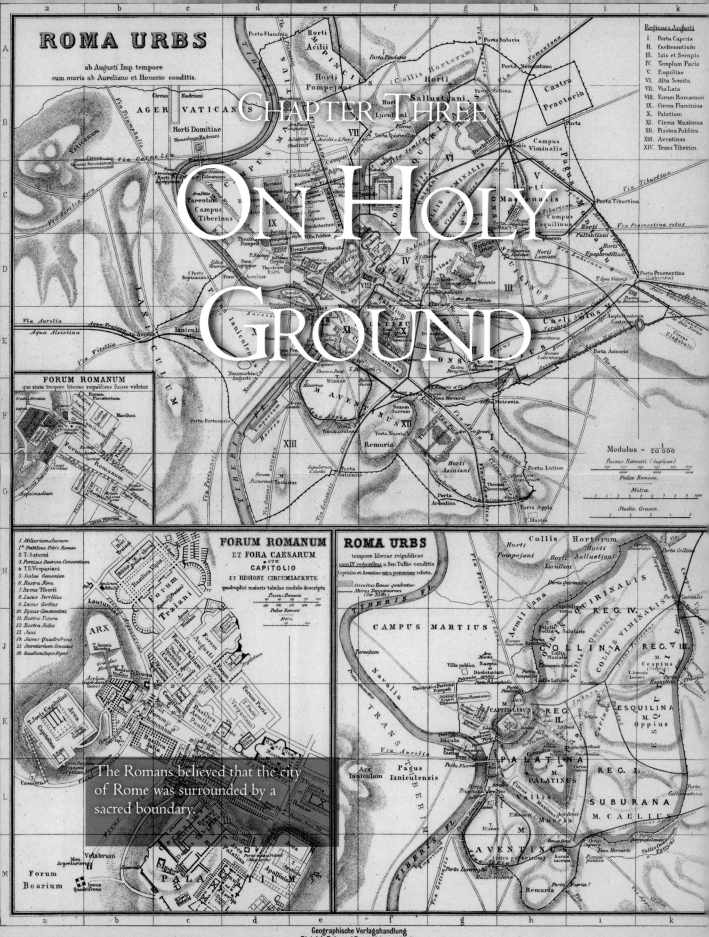

Chapter Three

On Holy Ground

The Romans believed that the city of Rome was surrounded by a sacred boundary.

"If any people ought to be allowed to consecrate their origins and refer them to a divine source, so great is the military glory of the Roman People that when they profess that their Father and the Father of their Founder was none other than Mars, the nations of the earth may well submit to this also with as good a grace as they submit to Rome's dominion."

—Livy

In the legend of Romulus and Remus, it is no mistake that the abandoned infants are nurtured by a woodpecker and a wolf: these animals were associated with their father, Mars. Romans related to the origin myth of their city because it reflected the nature of the empire. Conquests expanded the empire, but agriculture sustained that growth.

All across Rome, temples and other sacred spaces coexisted alongside homes, public baths, and other everyday structures. This intermingling of the common and the sacred reflects the Romans' core religious beliefs. Their faith was woven into the fabric of daily life.

ROME: THE CITY AS SPIRITUAL CENTER

Rome itself was in many ways considered a sacred site, chosen by deities and heroes long ago as a place of greatness. One sign of the city's religious character was the pomerium that enclosed it. This boundary was a strip of land that set off the city as a sacred place. It was marked at every change of direction by 6-foot-tall (1.8-meter-tall) blocks of stone. Any emperor who enlarged the empire was allowed to also enlarge the pomerium, and this was done on several occasions. When the Romans founded a colony, its pomerium was laid out just like Rome's. After the auspices were taken, the founder of the colony ceremonially plowed a furrow around the location. This procedure showed that colonies were intended to be "little Romes" where, among other things, the Roman deities would be honored. Whether in the capital or the colonies, burials were not allowed within the pomerium, for they would contaminate the holy ground.

Houses of the Gods

In his great epic the *Aeneid*, the poet Virgil included an episode in which the hero, Aeneas, is shown important landmarks of what will someday be the city of Rome. Among the sights is a hill covered with tangled thickets. Despite its wild and uninviting aspect, Aeneas is aware of the "god-haunted feel of the place."

After Rome was founded, this hill became the location of the Capitol, the great temple of Jupiter, Juno, and Minerva, together known as the Capitoline Triad. Many cities throughout the empire also came to have Capitols, dedicated to the same three deities. A Capitol was nearly always built on a hill or rise, generally close to the city's forum, or political center.

Inside the Capitol were statues of each member of the Triad. Each statue stood in its own cella, or room. Most temples, however, were dedicated to only one deity and so had only one cella. Classical Roman temples were rectangular in shape and elevated on a high platform called a podium, which might have storage areas beneath it. At the front of the temple, a wide stairway led from the ground to the top of the podium. Here there was a columned porch, sometimes taking up as much as half the temple's length. The cella, enclosed by solid walls at the back and sides, was behind the porch.

The architect Vitruvius, writing during the reign of Augustus, recommended that, whenever possible, temples and statues face west:

> This will enable those who approach the altar with offerings or sacrifices to face the direction of the sunrise in facing the statue in the temple, and thus those who are undertaking vows look toward the quarter from which the sun comes forth, and likewise the statues themselves appear to be coming forth out of the east to look upon them as they pray and sacrifice.

The Temple of Vesta

A few Roman temples were circular. The Temple of Vesta was built in this shape because it was intended to resemble the round huts in which the earliest Romans lived. Hercules also had a small, circular temple in Rome. A much grander building, though, was the Pantheon, a temple like no other. Behind its porch was a huge **rotunda**, roofed with a spectacular dome. In the center of the dome was a wide circular opening to let in sunlight. The lofty dome was probably intended to represent the sky, with the opening symbolizing the sun. The deities worshipped in the Pantheon may have been those after whom the planets were named—we know that Venus and Mars, at least, were honored there.

When Two Worshippers Was a Crowd

Temples of the Roman state religion were not meant to hold groups of worshippers. An individual could go into a temple to honor the deity privately, burning incense or leaving an offering on a small altar before the statue of the goddess or god. Public, group worship took place outside the temple, focusing on an altar erected at the foot of the stairs. This was where all blood sacrifices performed at the temple took place. (Blood sacrifices had to be conducted outdoors, under the open sky.) Only the priest spoke during the ceremony; everyone else participated with their minds and hearts, but not with their voices.

All temples had altars, but altars did not need to be at temples. Families had small altars in their homes and, quite often, outdoor altars on their property for blood sacrifices. Travelers sometimes set up roadside altars to thank a deity for protection on a journey. Some altars were part of open-air **shrines**, such as those dedicated to the Lares at crossroads in Rome. Small public altars were used for incense and other bloodless offerings.

Two very important altars—used for blood sacrifices—were the Ara Pacis, the "Altar of Peace," and the Ara Maxima, the "Greatest Altar." Both were located in Rome. The Ara Pacis was an impressive monument, dedicated by the emperor Augustus in 9 BCE. Made of marble, it was U-shaped and surrounded with a nearly square wall, 23 feet (7 m) high, that had openings on the east and west sides. A low podium supported this whole complex. Both altar and wall were adorned with wonderful sculptured **reliefs** that included images of Mother Earth, the emperor and his family, an episode from the story of Aeneas, and other legendary and ceremonial scenes.

The Ara Maxima was probably called the "Greatest" because of its ancientness. It was dedicated to Hercules, who was said to have set it up himself, making the first sacrifice at it. This altar was a place where businessmen often met to agree on deals, and where merchants sometimes came to pledge a tenth of their profits to Hercules. Women were not allowed to approach the Ara Maxima because, according to one legend, a priestess of Bona Dea ("The Good Goddess") once refused to give Hercules a drink of water from the goddess's sacred spring.

Diana, the goddess of the hunt and the moon

OUTDOOR WORSHIP

Many places and objects in the natural world had a religious significance. Sources of rivers, hot springs, groves of trees, and the like were felt to be holy places, where divine powers were strongly present. Worshippers might set up shrines or altars to deities on these sites, or there could even be full-blown temples. For example, we know of a few temples that were located in sacred groves outside of Rome. Most famous was the sanctuary of Diana in the wood of Nemi. The temple was built beside a small lake inside the grove, about 16 miles (25.7 kilometers) from Rome. Archaeologists have found numerous clay figurines at the site, left as offerings by grateful worshippers.

Another much-loved sacred site was the source of the Clitumnus River, a tributary of the Tiber. The author-senator Pliny the Younger has left us this description:

> There is a fair-sized hill, dark with ancient cypress-woods. Beneath this the spring rises, gushing out in several veins of unequal size. After the initial flow has smoothed out, it spreads into a broad pool, pure and clear as glass, so that you can count the coins that have been thrown into it … Near it there is an ancient and venerable temple. In it stands [an image of] Clitumnus himself, clothed, and draped in a crimson-bordered robe … Around this temple there are several smaller shrines, each with its god. Every one has its own cult [worship dedicated to it], its own name, and some even their own springs.

The Romans firmly believed that every place had a guardian spirit, its *genius loci,* "the spirit of the place." Sometimes, as with Clitumnus, the name of the genius was known; sometimes it was not. Either way, the Romans believed that these powers should be honored. Many soldiers stationed at outposts in the provinces seem to have been particularly careful to honor such spirits. Archaeologists have found a number of altars dedicated to the "genius of this place" at forts on the empire's frontiers. But with or without temples, altars, shrines, or statues, the presence of the divine in nature remained clear to many Romans.

The First Temple

Livy, a famous Roman historian, recorded the mythical foundation of the empire's first temple. According to his book *The History of Rome*:

[Romulus] then led his victorious army back, and being not more splendid in his deeds than willing to display them, he arranged the spoils of the enemy's dead commander upon a frame, suitably fashioned for the purpose, and, carrying it himself, mounted the Capitol. Having there deposited his burden, by an oak which the shepherds held sacred, at the same time as he made his offering he marked out the limits of a temple to Jupiter, and bestowed a title upon him. "Jupiter Feretrius," he said, "to thee I, victorious Romulus, myself a king, bring the panoply of a king, and dedicate a sacred precinct within the bounds which I have even now marked off in my mind, to be a seat for the spoils of honour which men shall bear hither in time to come, following my example, when they have slain kings and commanders of the enemy."

The story of Romulus set a precedent for the establishment of temples to commemorate conquest. It was common for generals to build temples at the site of their victories. In fact, conquest often provided the funding for building projects like temples.

Chapter Four
Spiritual
Men

A pontiff was a priest who oversaw religious and bureaucratic matters in the city of Rome.

"After making his vows on the Capitolium, the consul Publius Licinius set out from the city, wearing the general's cloak ... This event is always conducted with great dignity and solemnity."
—Livy on the religious ceremonies associated with war

Romans had a clear vision of a man's responsibilities. For free men, these responsibilities included acting as the head of their household, or the *pater familias* (the father of the family). Fathers were in charge of both their children and their wives. Roman men, therefore, played a key role in ceremonies such as weddings and funerals.

The ruling elite saw the entirety of the empire as a kind of extended family. Societal conventions encouraged rulers to make decisions with the best interests of their subjects in mind. Religion and politics were intertwined in ancient Rome. In fact, many prominent figures served as priests as one aspect of their political careers. And whether a man was *pater patriae*—the father of the country (ruler of the empire)—or pater familias, he had the responsibility of ensuring that everyone who depended on him would enjoy the peace of the gods.

WORSHIP AT HOME

It was a father's duty to lead home-based worship, acting as a priest for his entire household, including slaves as well as family members. He was responsible for maintaining a lararium, the family shrine to the Lares. This could be a freestanding shrine, a wall niche, or even a painting on the wall. In well-to-do homes, it was generally located in the garden, kitchen, or **atrium**, which was something like a modern living room. Some men, including the emperor Augustus, also had a lararium in their bedroom. One of the first things a pater familias did after getting up in the morning was light incense at the lararium, and he might worship the Lares in this way again at bedtime.

At dinnertime, the family honored the Lares, Penates, and the goddess Vesta.

This lararium features an image of Minerva.

Traditionally, the whole household gathered in front of the lararium to call on the deities before going to the table. After the appetizer course, the family was silent while the father made an offering by throwing mola salsa and a choice piece of meat into the hearth fire or a small altar fire. These ancient customs were cherished by many Romans. The poet Horace, for example, wrote, "O, divine nights and meals where we eat, my family and I, before the Lar of my own home."

The pater familias was also responsible for maintaining a proper relationship between his family and the dead. In the lararium, or in another special place, he kept busts or wax masks of his ancestors. During the festival of Lemuria (May 9, 11, and 13), he had to make sure that unhappy ghosts would not harm the living. Each of the three nights, when everyone else was asleep, the pater familias got up, made a gesture against evil, and washed his hands. Then, barefoot, he walked through the house with nine black beans, food for the dead because beans were believed to contain a kind of life force of their own. He threw them back over his shoulder one at a time while chanting a prayer. When his task was done, this pious father could feel some assurance that the dead were satisfied and would not carry off any of his family to join them in the underworld.

PRIESTS OF THE STATE

As it was a father's duty to maintain the pax deorum for his family, other men took this responsibility on behalf of the state as a whole. First and foremost in this role was the emperor himself. He was the *pontifex maximus*, the chief priest and head of the state religion. All other priests in the city were appointed by the emperor, and they held their positions for life. These men were wealthy, educated senators, whose religious duties were only part time.

About one-quarter to one-third of Roman senators served as priests. This mix of priesthood and politics may seem odd to us, but it made perfect sense to the Romans. As Cicero explained:

> Among the many things … that our ancestors created and established under divine inspiration, nothing is more renowned than their decision to entrust the worship of the gods and the highest interests of the state to the same men—so that the most eminent and illustrious citizens might ensure the maintenance of religion by the proper administration of the state, and the maintenance of the state by the prudent interpretation of religion.

Piety and Fatherliness in Roman Literature

The model of Roman manhood was Aeneas. In Virgil's *Aeneid*, the hero is frequently called "pious Aeneas" because of his supreme devotion to duty. A favorite subject in Roman art was Aeneas carrying his weak and aged father away from the conquered city of Troy. Aeneas's pietas toward his father was only surpassed by his pietas toward Jupiter, the father of the gods. At every turn, the hero followed the god's will, even when it caused him great personal unhappiness. Having fled the destruction of the Trojan War, he knew that his duty was to follow Jupiter's guidance and find a new home for himself and all who depended on him.

Aeneas's fatherly concern for his people mirrored the fatherliness of Jupiter. Fatherliness, even in literature, was one of the most valued qualities in ancient Rome. It was expected especially from leaders, whether in the government, the army, the local community, or the family, so it isn't surprising to see it appear in one of our most treasured works of Roman literature.

The city of Rome had sixteen priests called **pontiffs** (in **Latin**, *pontifices*). They oversaw such matters as adoptions, wills, and burials. Traditionally, they were also in charge of the calendar (setting the dates of movable holidays, for example) and of recordkeeping for the city. Mainly, though, they were experts in religious law. They made sure that government officials who had religious duties performed them properly, and they also oversaw "all the priesthoods" and their helpers "to make sure that they commit no error in regard to the sacred laws," as historian Dionysius of Halicarnassus wrote. He added, "For private citizens who are not knowledgeable about religious matters concerning the gods and divine spirits, the pontifices are explainers and interpreters." Rome's pontiffs could exercise authority in nearby towns and cities, but not in the provinces. Roman colonies had their own pontiffs as well as augurs.

Fifteen priests known as flamens also belonged to the college, or association, of pontiffs. Each flamen served one particular deity. Most important was the Flamen Dialis, the priest of Jupiter. Unlike the other flamens, he had to follow a number of ancient rules. For example, he could not touch a dead body, he could not be absent from Rome for longer than several days at a time, and he had to have been married only once and in the most formal type of wedding ceremony. His wife, the Flaminica Dialis, assisted him in some of his duties and had to follow the same rules. Other Italian towns, as well as Roman colonies, also had flamens. In addition, priests who looked after the worship of the deified emperors, both in Rome and the provinces, were called flamens.

The augurs formed another major priestly college. They interpreted the will of the gods and laid out sacred space. The college had sixteen members, one of whom was the emperor. There were several other priesthoods in Rome. Among them was the twelve-member Arval Brotherhood, which performed regular sacrifices for the health of the emperor and his family. The Salii were twenty-four priests of Mars, famous for the leaping dances they performed at certain festivals in the god's honor.

Most priests of the state religion were not assigned to serve in any particular temple. Each temple, however, had its own custodian living next to it. If an individual wanted to make a sacrifice at the temple, the custodian was the one who would arrange it. In addition, he was in charge of looking after the building and had a staff of servants and slaves to do the actual work of keeping the temple clean and in good repair. Many temples also had gatekeepers, clerks, guides for visitors, and other workers.

MEN OF MYSTERY

Many men were drawn to the mystery religions. Some were initiated into the Mysteries of Demeter and Persephone, others became priests of Cybele, and still others, like Apuleius, devoted themselves to Isis. But perhaps the most popular mystery religion for men was that of Mithras. In fact, only men were allowed to become initiates of Mithras. The god was particularly attractive to soldiers, who carried Mithraism (along with traditional Roman religion) throughout the empire.

Although Mithras was originally a Persian god, his worship in the Roman Empire took on its own unique form. Its ceremonies were secret, but literature and archaeology have revealed some information. Group worship took place in caves or small cavelike rooms. A bull sacrifice played a major role, since Mithras had slain a great bull in order to give life to the earth. There were also rites of purification and ceremonial meals of bread and water, or perhaps wine mixed with water. Initiates of Mithras progressed through seven ranks, known as Raven, Bridegroom, Soldier, Lion, Persian, Sun

Runner, and Father. Each of these was associated with a planet, and astrology seems to have played some role in Mithraism. But as with the other mystery religions (and even with some aspects of Rome's state religion), it is almost impossible for scholars today to know or understand many details of the worshippers' beliefs and practices.

A flamen

CHAPTER FIVE

RELIGIOUS WOMEN

Vestal Virgins, a 1727 painting
by Jean Raoux

"A vestal virgin is stretching out towards you her suppliant hands, those same hands which she is accustomed to stretch out, on your behalf, to the immortal gods. Consider how dangerous, how arrogant a deed it would be for you to reject her entreaties ..."

—Cicero

Although women in ancient Rome did not have many legal rights or political power, a number of women made their mark as priestesses. Becoming a priestess was an honor accompanied by additional rights and some political sway. Not every cult included priestesses, though. Many of the cults that featured priestesses were associated with goddesses rather than gods, demonstrating the divide between the men and women of the empire.

Everyday Roman women were expected to worship according to the dictates of their husband or father. Yet there is evidence that women sometimes worshipped independently of men in their homes. Roman culture also included festivals dedicated to mothers. During these festivals, women made offerings to goddesses on their own.

Surprisingly, the lives of priestesses are often better documented than the lives of average women; ancient Roman writers did not think that women's experiences were worth documenting.

THE VESTAL VIRGINS

As we have seen, political leadership and religious leadership were closely related. Although we know of a few examples of women in public office in cities in Roman-ruled Greece and Asia Minor, there were no government positions open to women in Rome itself. As a result, the roles they could play in the state religion were quite limited. For example, women were rarely, if ever, allowed to preside over blood sacrifices. However, Rome had one priesthood of women that was considered all important to the well-being of the city and empire. The women of this priesthood were known as vestal virgins.

There were six vestal virgins. Chosen for their office between the ages of six and ten, they were from upper-class families and had to be physically perfect and have both parents still living. They went to live at the House of Vesta in the Forum, where they would spend a total of thirty years: ten being trained, ten actively performing religious duties, and ten teaching the younger vestals. During this time, they could not have any relationships with men. If they did, they were put on trial by the pontiffs and executed if found guilty. After their thirty years of service, they were free to return to their family homes and get married. Most, however, chose to remain in the House of Vesta. As Dionysius of Halicarnassus observed, "The vestal virgins receive many fine honors from the city and do not therefore yearn for children or marriage."

Vestals did enjoy privileges that most other Roman women did not. A vestal was freed from her father's authority and could make a will and give legal testimony without a guardian's oversight. Like a male officeholder, a vestal had an attendant called a lictor walk before her when she went out. If she happened to come upon a criminal being led to execution, he was immediately pardoned because of the power of her sacred presence. Prime seats were even reserved for the vestals in the theater. The state paid them a salary that covered

The Sibyls and Skepticism

Attempts at divining the future were important in ancient Rome, particularly during times of uncertainty or war. Prior to the establishment of the empire (when Rome was still ruled by kings), Tarquin the Elder acquired a set of texts called the Sibylline Books. These books were oracles recorded by a prophetess, or "sibyl," called the Sibyl of Cumae. The Sibylline Books remained popular over the course of the empire, and later sibyls added books of their own. Yet books were not automatically considered true prophecies. Sibylline Books had to be evaluated carefully, and there was a process in place. According to the historian Tacitus, a priest named Gallus ignored the process and introduced a motion in the Senate through a young senator to recognize a new volume:

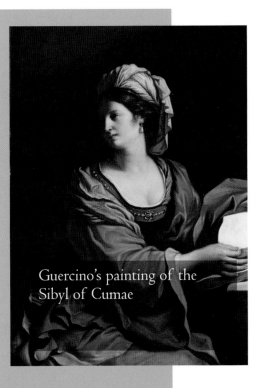

Guercino's painting of the Sibyl of Cumae

A motion was next brought forward in the Senate by Quintilianus, a tribune of the people, respecting an alleged book of the Sibyl. Caninius Gallus, a member of the College of the Fifteen [a group of priests], had asked that it might be received among the other volumes of the same prophetess by a decree on the subject. This having been carried by a division, the emperor sent a letter in which he gently censured the tribune, as ignorant of ancient usage because of his youth. Gallus he scolded for having introduced the matter in a thin Senate, notwithstanding his long experience in the science of religious ceremonies, without taking the opinion of the College or having the verses read and criticised, as was usual, by its presidents, though their authenticity was very doubtful.

all their living expenses and then some. The vestal virgins, in fact, made up Rome's only full-time, paid priesthood.

These honors came to the vestals because their duties were believed to guarantee the health and safety of the state. They participated in important processions and ceremonies. They made the mola salsa that was used in major sacrifices. They guarded the city's most ancient holy objects, said to have been brought from Troy by Aeneas himself. Most important, the vestals tended the eternal flame of the sacred fire in the Temple of Vesta. This was the hearth fire of all Romans, and as long as it continued to burn, Rome would stay strong.

OTHER PRIESTESSES

Just as many emperors were deified after death, so were some empresses, and honor might be paid to an empress's iuno just as to an emperor's genius. Some women in the imperial family acted as priestesses in the worship of the deified emperors and empresses. It appears that quite a few women in the eastern part of the empire, and even in some Italian towns, were priestesses responsible for honoring the imperial genius and iuno. Such women were leading citizens of their communities. They were also extremely wealthy—part of their priestly role involved paying for sacrifices, religious festivals, and public entertainments. Often these women's husbands also served in the imperial worship, but it seems that many or most of the priestesses held their titles and offices in their own right.

In Greece and Asia Minor, women could be priestesses of Greek gods or goddesses, especially of Artemis, goddess of women, mothers, the moon, and the wilderness. These same women often served in the imperial worship as well. The city of Perge in Asia Minor erected a statue to Plancia Magna, with an **inscription** on its base reading:

Priestesses were members of the upper class and were afforded great respect.

Priestess of Artemis

and both first and sole public priestess

of the mother of the gods

for the duration of her life

pious and patriotic

Plancia Magna gave her city a magnificent entrance gate that was decorated with statues and inscriptions honoring two deified emperors, a deified empress, and the reigning emperor and empress.

Women involved in the Mysteries of Demeter, Bacchus, Cybele, and Isis sometimes had the opportunity to become priestesses. Even those who did not take these leadership roles could still dedicate themselves to their beloved deity through initiation. Isis was especially attractive to women, who were given more respect and authority in the worship of this goddess than in any other sphere of Roman life. Isis was called the goddess of women, and at least one hymn to her proclaimed that she made women equal to men. She also embraced all social classes, including slaves and ex-slaves.

Isis was worshipped not only in private initiations but also in public ceremonies. For example, people gathered at her temple in Rome to sing hymns every day as the doors were being opened in the morning and closed in the afternoon. And here is Apuleius's description of some of the women participating in a procession during a festival of Isis:

Women glowing in their white vestments moved with symbolic gestures of delight. Blossomy with the chaplets [wreathes] of the Spring, they scattered flowerets out of the aprons of their dresses … Others, who bore polished mirrors on their backs, walked before [the statue of] the Goddess and reflected all the people coming-after as if they were advancing towards the Image. Others, again, carrying combs of ivory, went through the various caressive motions of combing and dressing the queenly tresses of their Lady; or they sprinkled the street with drops of unguent [perfumed oil] … Then there came walking a great band of men and women of all classes and ages, who had been initiated into the Mysteries of the Goddess and who were all clad in linen garments of the purest white.

Women's religious activities were not limited to priesthoods or to the Mysteries. Although fathers played the main role in family worship, mothers did take part by tending the hearth, taking care of the lararium, and similar activities. Women could attend sacrifices and other public ceremonies of the state religion, even if their only role (as for most of the other people present) was to watch and keep silent. There were many goddesses whom women particularly favored and who were especially concerned with women's lives. On special occasions and in times of need, women commonly prayed and made offerings at the temples of these much-loved goddesses. In spite of limited primary-source texts about women in ancient Rome, it seems clear that many Roman women had rich religious experiences.

CHAPTER SIX

MARKING LIFE'S TRANSITIONS

An ancient headstone in the
Roman city of Chellah (modern-
day Rabat, Morocco)

> *"I lived for twenty-seven years, and I was married for sixteen years to the same man. After I gave birth to six children, only one of whom is still alive, I died."*
> —An epitaph for the wife of a legionnaire

Religion played a large role in most Romans' everyday lives, and like today, religious ceremonies also marked transitions through the stages of life. For instance, birthdays were important family occasions for Romans of all ages. Pliny the Elder explained that sacrificial pottage (porridge) was part of a birthday celebration. However, not all occasions were happy ones. Prayers, sacrifices, and rituals helped Romans navigate difficult births, deaths, and everything in between.

LIFE'S BEGINNINGS

In the ancient world, birth could be a dangerous and frightening experience. Medical knowledge was limited, so many mothers and babies died during or soon after birth. Infants born healthy might not stay that way for long: about 45 percent of Roman children did not reach their tenth birthday. Given this situation, parents often sought divine help to protect their children.

Women prayed to Diana, Juno Lucina, or a water goddess named Egeria to give them safe pregnancies, easy labors, and healthy babies. For several nights after the birth, three men of the household carried out a protective ceremony, striking the threshold with an axe, then with a pestle, then sweeping the threshold with a broom. The numina of these tools of civilization would defend the newborn from Silvanus and other wild spirits. For further divine protection, the family set up a bed for Juno and a table for Hercules in the atrium, as well as a table where the mother's friends could leave offerings for the gods.

Eight days after birth for a girl, and nine for a boy, the baby was purified and named. At this time, many Romans believed, goddesses of fate would decide the child's destiny. Family members were on the lookout for bolts of lightning or other signs from the gods that might give them a hint of what the baby's future held.

Every stage of a child's development was watched over or empowered by a particular deity or numen. There were, for example, Edusa and Potina to teach it to eat and drink; Ossipago and Carna to strengthen its bones and muscles; Fabulinus and Locutius to help it speak, first in single words and then in sentences; Numeria to help it learn to count; and Camena to teach it to sing.

Along with appealing to the appropriate deities or numina, parents had their children wear a round pendant called a bulla as protection against the destructive force of envy. Children also dressed in purple-bordered togas, like those worn by priests, to mark them as holy. And of course, parents were careful to teach their children proper pietas so that they would be able to do their part to maintain the pax deorum when they grew up.

Rites of Passage

At around sixteen, a boy had his coming-of-age. Roman families often chose to celebrate this occasion on March 17, the festival of Liber, a god concerned with the growth of both humans and crops. The boy put aside his childhood clothes and for the first time donned the white toga of manhood. He took off his bulla and left it in the lararium as an offering to the family's guardian spirits. Then he, his parents, and their friends went to the Forum, where he was formally enrolled as a citizen. At the Capitol, they made sacrifices to Jupiter and the goddess Iuventas (Youth). The celebration was completed with a feast held at the entrance to the family home— presumably so that everyone passing by would know the boy had become a man. The young man and his family celebrated again when he had his first shave, around the age of twenty-one. The shaved-off beard was offered to the Lares.

There was no coming-of-age ceremony for girls, who might marry as young as twelve. A wedding day had to be chosen carefully, because many days (including the entire month of May) were unlucky for beginning a marriage. The night before a girl's wedding, she gave her bulla to the Lares while her father made an offering of incense. At or before dawn the next day, her mother helped her dress in her bridal clothes, which included a straight white tunic and a red or orange-yellow veil. Her hair was arranged in a style said to symbolize modesty (it was the same hairstyle worn by the vestals), and she also wore a wreath of herbs and flowers that were considered lucky.

The wedding ceremony took place at the bride's home. It began with an animal sacrifice and could not continue until a haruspex examined the internal organs and announced that the gods approved of the marriage. Then a married woman joined together the right hands of the bride and groom, and they stated their consent to be married. A procession accompanied by singers, flute players, and torchbearers led the bride to the groom's house. He carried her over the threshold so that she would not stumble, which would foretell bad luck for the marriage. Next, the new wife ceremoniously offered her husband fire and water, symbols of the necessities of life and also of the elements that come together to create new life. After this, he presented her to his Lares, and then the wedding feast could begin.

Journey's End

People had different ideas about the reasons for life's difficulties. For some, it was a matter of fate. For others, what happened to them was simply due to random chance or luck. To the philosopher-emperor Marcus Aurelius, fate and luck operated together with the gods: "The work of the gods is full of Providence [Fate]: the work of Fortune is not divorced from nature or the spinning and winding of the threads ordained by Providence." Another popular opinion was that problems were the gods' way of testing and strengthening humans. To this idea, Seneca added, "It is not what you endure, but how you endure it that is important."

One way or another, though, death finally came to everyone. The spirit Caeculus took away the dead person's sight, and Viduus separated the soul from the body. Members of the household laid out the corpse, washed it, and perfumed it with cedar oil, honey, and myrrh. The body was then placed on a flower-decked bed in the atrium, where incense was constantly kept burning. Women were hired to lament the deceased, often to the accompaniment of flute players. After a week, the funeral procession set out for the family tomb. Escorting the deceased were musicians, torchbearers, and men carrying the masks or busts of the ancestors. The children of the dead person marched along dressed all in black.

At or near the tomb, the body was laid on a funeral pyre and cremated. Then family members sprinkled the ashes with wine and milk, dried them, and put them into a marble urn in the tomb. After circling the tomb three times and calling out a last farewell to the deceased, they returned home. They sacrificed a ram to the Lares, then shared the traditional funeral meal of eggs, beans, lentils, and chicken. For nine more days of mourning, none of the family did any work. At the end of this period, wine and milk were offered to the spirits of the dead, and then the survivors could resume their normal lives.

People had varying ideas about what happened after death. A common belief was that the spirits of the dead lived on in the underworld, which they could occasionally leave to interact with the living. These spirits were called the Manes (MAH-nays) or *divi parentes*, "divine ancestors." They were honored at major Roman festivals every year. However, some classicists maintain that inscriptions on tombs prove that the majority of Romans did not believe in the afterlife. Historian Valerie M. Warrior says, "Numerous tombstones express the finality of death by the letters 'nf f ns nc' (*non fui, fui, non sum, non curo*—I didn't exist, I did exist, I don't exist, I have no cares)."

In the House of Death

The *Aeneid* provides us with a closer look at the belief system of the ancient Romans. In the epic, Aeneas travels to the underworld to see his father, Anchises:

> But first go down to the House of Death, the Underworld,
>
> go through [Lake] Avernus' depths, my son, to seek me, meet me there.
>
> I am not condemned to wicked Tartarus, those bleak [spirits],
>
> I live in Elysium, the luminous fields where the true
>
> and faithful gather. A chaste Sibyl will guide you there,
>
> once you have offered the blood of many pure black sheep.

Anchises describes the two components of the underworld: Tartarus and Elysium. Tartarus equates loosely to the idea of hell, and Elysium equates to the idea of heaven. This conception of the underworld comes from Greek mythology, which demonstrates again the way the Romans wove together religious ideas from many cultures.

CHAPTER SEVEN

HOLIDAYS AND FESTIVALS

Chariot racing was a popular way of honoring the gods.

"The altar was content to give off smoke from Sabine herbs, and laurel was burned with no small sound. If there was anyone who could add violets to garlands made from meadow flowers, he was a rich man!"

—Ovid

Holidays and festivals were plentiful in ancient Rome. Religious observances were an integral part of just about every aspect of life, even during *ludi*, or games. For many Romans during the time of the emperors, these races and shows were more important as a source of entertainment than as a religious observance. Nevertheless, the religious aspect of the games was made clear by the processions that began the events. Before a day of chariot racing, "floats" with statues of various deities entered the circus, or stadium, and went around the track. Honoring the gods with games was one of the traditional ways of reinforcing the pax deorum.

Public and Private Celebrations

There were many religious observances throughout the year. Some were full-blown festivals lasting an entire day or more, when no business was conducted and people gathered together for ceremonies and celebrations. Other occasions were half-day holidays. Most festivals occurred on the same date every year, but some were "movable feasts" (like modern Easter) whose exact date each year had to be set by the pontiffs. Unscheduled festivals could be declared, too—for example, to celebrate a military victory. Most official holidays fell on odd-numbered days, which were considered luckiest. State holidays were celebrated publicly with sacrifices and often with ludi. Admission was free, and vast crowds attended.

The Romans also recognized private holidays, which were family occasions, such as birthdays. (The emperor's birthday, however, called for a grand public celebration.) All important family events were generally marked by prayers to the Lares and Penates. In addition, families gave special worship to these spirits on the first of each month (called the Kalends), roughly a week later (the Nones), and in the middle of the month (the Ides). On these days, the mother decorated the hearth with flower garlands, and the father burned incense and made other offerings to the family guardians. Typical offerings, especially on the Kalends, were honeycombs, grapes, and cakes.

A CALENDAR OF FESTIVITIES

Many Roman holidays are difficult to understand today, even for scholars. People often wonder what a particular holiday was about, what its meaning was, or what worshippers were seeking through their actions. In a number of cases, by the time of the emperors the answers to these questions had been forgotten by the Romans themselves. For most Romans, it was enough to know that their ancestors had celebrated these same holidays, with the same ceremonies, for generation after generation. One of the best ways to maintain the pax deorum was to keep tradition alive.

All the same, at least some of the reasons for a number of the year's festivities seem clear. For example, the names of many of the months can tell us a lot about what deities were especially honored then and what types of ceremonies took place. The agricultural cycle was also extremely important because even the most city-bred Romans were well aware that they depended on the earth's production of crops.

January was named after Janus, the god of beginnings, gates, and doorways. His festival, January 1, marked the start of the new year. People celebrated by giving one another small gifts and were careful to speak only of good things all day. On January 3,

An artist's rendering of a music festival in Pompeii

the Arval Brotherhood vowed sacrifices to the Capitoline Triad and other deities for the well-being of the emperor and his family during the coming year; they also carried out the sacrifices that they had vowed the previous January. Around the same time, Compitalia was celebrated so that people could honor the Lares of the crossroads. January 11 brought Carmentalia, dedicated to Carmentis, a goddess who presided over birth. Toward the end of the month came Sementivae, a country festival that prepared seeds for sowing, with prayers and sacrifices to Ceres and Mother Earth.

Februa meant "offerings or ceremonies for purification," and this was a theme in February's major festivals. February 15 was Lupercalia. Priests called Luperci (literally, "wolfmen") made a sacrifice at the place where Rome's founder, Romulus, and his brother, Remus, were said to have been nursed by a wolf after being abandoned in the wilderness. Following the sacrifice, the Luperci, clothed in goatskin, ran through the streets of Rome. Crowds turned out to watch them, and they struck everyone they met with goatskin thongs. This was an act of purification, and people also believed that it would help women who were having trouble becoming pregnant.

Roman festivals sometimes overlapped one another, and Lupercalia came in the middle of Parentalia, February 13–21. The dead were said to wander freely during Parentalia. Temples were closed, but people set out offerings of food and flowers for the dead and held feasts at the tombs of their ancestors. Then, on the twenty-second, Caristia was devoted to renewing family ties, patching up quarrels, and honoring the Lares.

Mars was the namesake of March, when his priests performed their leaping dance on two different holidays and military trumpets were purified. April seems to have been Venus's month and was the favorite time for Roman weddings. In the countryside, agricultural activities were really getting under way, so April also saw a number of festivals related to the earth and farming—for example, the seven-day Cerialia, devoted to the grain goddess Ceres. April 21 was Parilia, in rural Italy a festival to honor the divine guardian of shepherds and their flocks. This was also the official date of Rome's founding, so in the city people celebrated Rome's birthday. Both the rural and urban festivities featured bonfires that people leaped over for good luck.

Floralia, the feast of the flower goddess Flora, began on April 28 and lasted through May 3. May was named after Maia, a goddess of growing things. She was said by some to be the mother of Mercury, who shared a festival with Jupiter on May 15. Before this, however, came Lemuria, when fathers protected their households from troublesome ghosts. The end of the month

Why Phoebus's Raven Cannot Drink

Ovid's *Fasti* is a multivolume poem that describes Roman holidays and festivals. It also recounts the myths attached to these celebrations. Though Ovid never finished *Fasti*, the surviving volumes provide a rare look at Roman mythology. In this excerpt, the god Phoebus (also known as Apollo) employs the help of a raven to prepare for religious rites:

Ovid (43 BCE–17 CE)

> It happened that Phoebus was preparing a formal festival for Jupiter … "Go on, my bird," said he, "and so that nothing may hold up the holy rites, bring clear water from living springs." The raven lifts a gilded bowl with his hooked feet and, rising high, flies on his mission through the air.
>
> There was a fig-tree standing thickly covered with fruit that was still hard. He tests it with his beak, but it wasn't ready for picking. Forgetting his orders, he is said to have sat beneath the tree waiting for the fruit to become sweet in the slow passage of time.

As punishment for the bird's failure (and his subsequent lie to Phoebus about why he didn't complete his task), Phoebus says that the raven will never again drink from a spring.

brought Ambarvalia. For this festival of purification, people called on Ceres, Bacchus, Jupiter, Mars, and Janus. To drive away harmful forces, farmers led a sheep, a pig, and an ox around the boundary of their fields; in the city, the same three animals were led around the pomerium. The animals were then sacrificed, and the rest of the day was spent in feasting and merrymaking.

So the year went, each month with its festivals to honor the gods, the land, and the history of Rome. The year ended with the most joyous holiday of all, Saturnalia. It began on December 17 and continued through the twenty-third. On the first day, there was a sacrifice at the temple of Saturn with a public feast afterward. During the festival, people wore bright-colored clothes, went to parties, exchanged gifts and good wishes, and gave their slaves time off. The author Macrobius recorded that, in addition, "Households faithful to the rites honour their slaves by serving them dishes first as if they were the masters." Everyone wore a soft felt cap like the one that was traditionally given to freed slaves, perhaps to show that during this time of year, at least, all human beings were equal. The festival was held in honor of the god Saturn, who was said to have been the first ruler of Italy, the one who gave people laws and taught them how to plant crops.

WOMEN'S FESTIVALS

Some Roman holidays were mainly for women, or involved their active participation. This was especially true for **matrons**—freeborn married women—particularly those in the upper class. The holiday of Matronalia, on March 1, was dedicated to them and was rather like Mothers' Day. Women received gifts from their husbands and children; during the reign of Vespasian, the emperor himself gave presents to Rome's matrons. The women visited Juno's temple and offered flowers there.

Religion in the Roman Empire

The first of April was the Veneralia, and matrons went to the temple of Venus Verticordia, "Turner of Hearts," who strengthened marriages. Worshippers washed and dressed Venus's statue in the temple and drank a beverage made of milk, honey, and poppy seeds. Also on April 1, lower-class women honored Fortuna Virilis, the goddess of the Luck of Men, with ceremonies held in public bathhouses. The goddess of the Luck of Women—Fortuna Muliebris—doesn't seem to have had a particular holiday. But the empress Livia, Augustus's wife, was especially devoted to her and renovated her temple just outside of Rome.

The Vestalia arrived on June 9. On this occasion, Roman matrons took offerings to the Temple of Vesta and were allowed into the holiest part of it, usually open only to the vestal virgins. The Matralia on June 11 was the day of Mater Matuta, Mother of the Dawn. Matrons celebrated it with their sisters and prayed for the well-being of one anothers' children. On August 13, there was a festival of Diana. Women wearing flower garlands went in a torchlit procession to Diana's sanctuary in the grove of Nemi to thank her for answered prayers.

December 3 brought the festival of Bona Dea (the Good Goddess), which matrons and the vestal virgins celebrated in the home of a leading government official. All males, including children and slaves, had to leave before preparations could even begin. Then the official's wife or mother decorated the house with vines and other greenery. Priestesses of Bona Dea, who were ex-slaves, brought the statue of the goddess from her temple for the occasion and probably also took part in the ceremonies. These were held at night, and the celebration included a feast, music, singing, and dancing. Many people believed that if these festivities were disturbed or interrupted, the well-being of all Romans would be endangered.

CHAPTER EIGHT

HARMONY AND DISCORD

While the Roman Empire was known for religious tolerance, at times the government persecuted believers of minority religions, like the Druids.

"I am convinced that Romulus by his auspices and Numa by his establishment of ritual laid the foundation of our state, which assuredly could never have been as great as it is had we not maintained the fullest measure of divine favor."

—Cicero

Romans were mostly known for their religious tolerance, and as the empire expanded, so did the pantheon of gods. Rome's religion developed over centuries, and was continuously evolving. With their value for tradition, the Romans rarely dropped time-honored religious practices, but they generally had no problem adding on new gods, new holidays, and new ceremonies or prayers. When Rome conquered a territory, often the deities of that place were formally invited to join the Roman gods. Usually the residents of conquered lands were permitted to continue their own traditional worship. Emperors even instructed provincial governors to preserve the local holy places.

Religion in Flux

Under Roman influence, the native deities of many provinces underwent a transformation, becoming more Roman themselves. This happened most obviously in Gaul (modern France and Belgium) and Britain. Before conquest, people in these provinces seldom carved stone images of their deities. After conquest, sculptures of British and Gaulish deities became quite common. The gods and goddesses were frequently portrayed wearing Roman clothing and hairstyles. Often they received Roman names as well, added to their original name and based on the Roman deity to whom they seemed most similar. So, for example, the British goddess Sul became Sul Minerva. A great many British and Gaulish gods were identified with Mars, Mercury, Jupiter, and Apollo, resulting in "combination gods" such as Mars Camulos, Mercury Artaios, Jupiter Taranis, and Apollo Belenus.

One thing that Roman authorities could not accept either in the provinces or at home was a threat to order. There was a difference between religion, which followed proper forms, and superstition. To the Romans, superstition was irrational, overly emotional devotion that resulted in worshippers thinking more of themselves and the otherworld than of the community and this world. This posed one kind of threat. Another came from religious groups, such as the Mysteries, that had their own organization independent of the state. Emperors often feared that any group—religious or otherwise—with its own leaders and treasury might oppose government authority or even start a rebellion. A few religious communities, it seems, did in fact agitate to overthrow Roman rule in some provinces. For all these reasons, emperors from time to time tried to suppress (often violently) or regulate various religious groups, including Isis worshippers, the Druid priesthood of Gaul and Britain, and Christians.

A MARRIAGE OF "CHURCH" AND STATE

When Jesus of Nazareth said, "Render to Caesar the things that are Caesar's, and to God the things that are God's," he was expressing a separation of government and religion that was totally new. For the ancient Romans, it was perfectly natural for religion and politics to mix. As we have seen, they firmly believed that proper worship of the gods was necessary for the well-being of the city and the entire empire. Participating in the public ceremonies of the state religion was an act of patriotism. Refusing to take part in these rites could be seen as an act of treason. This attitude was problematic for Jews and Christians, who acknowledged only one god and often felt that participating in Roman ceremonies was a betrayal of their beliefs.

The Roman authorities tended to be more tolerant of Jews than of Christians. Even though Jewish beliefs and practices were very different from Roman ones, Judaism was understandable as the traditional religion of a particular people. Nevertheless, there were individuals in the Roman Empire who were terribly prejudiced, even to the point of violence, against Jews. And when the Jewish province of Judaea rebelled against Roman rule in 66–73 CE, the empire was merciless. Roman troops destroyed the Temple in Jerusalem, the Jews' most sacred place, forever changing the nature of Jewish religious practice.

Christianity was a new religion, without the respectability of a long history. Moreover, Christians actively worked to convince people to join them. This sort of thing had been almost unknown in the Greco-Roman world, and many people were highly offended by Christian efforts to make converts. Some Christians were very vocal about their contempt for traditional Roman religion, and some made a public point of refusing to honor the gods and the emperor's genius. To make matters worse, there were a few Christians who preached that the empire was evil and had to be destroyed so that the kingdom of God could be established on earth. When Roman authorities encountered such ideas, they decided that Christians were dangerous rebels.

Christians were first persecuted during the reign of the emperor Nero (54–68 CE), when he accused them of starting a fire that destroyed more than half of the city of Rome.

Tacitus described what happened next:

People who admitted their belief were arrested, and then later, through their information, a huge crowd was convicted not so much of the crime of setting the fire, as of hating humankind. Mockery was heaped upon them as they were killed … Nero offered his garden for this spectacle and provided circus entertainment where he put on a chariot driver's outfit and mingled with the crowd or stood in a chariot. And so pity arose, even for those who were guilty … since they seemed to have been slaughtered not for public good but to satisfy the cruelty of one man.

Fortunately, such persecutions were relatively rare, at least in the first two centuries CE, when Christians made up a very small percentage of the empire's population, and Roman authorities were generally content to leave them alone so long as they didn't cause any trouble.

THE LEGACY OF THE GODS

Most Romans felt that Jews and Christians were extremely intolerant to insist on the existence and worship of only one god. Traditional Roman religion, along with the Mysteries, remained strong throughout the 300s. By the 320s, however, the emperor Constantine was favoring Christianity over other religions. All but one of the emperors who came after him were Christians. Still, the vast majority of the empire's residents remained true to their ancient beliefs and practices. Emperors resorted to various techniques, including violence and persecution, to make their subjects convert to Christianity. In 391,

Dionysius of Halicarnassus on Assimilation

Dionysius was a writer originally from Halicarnassus (in Greece). He spent more than two decades writing a history of Rome called *Roman Antiquities*. In the book, Dionysius discusses the complicated relationship between Rome and foreign gods. Even though we know that Rome incorporated the gods of other cultures into mainstream worship, it seems like the process of "official" assimilation required endorsement—sometimes from oracles:

> Notwithstanding the influx into Rome of innumerable foreigners who are under great obligation to worship their ancestral gods in accordance with the customs of their own countries, the city has never officially emulated any foreign practices. But, even though Rome has imported certain rites on the recommendation of oracles, she celebrates them in accordance with her own traditions, banishing all mythical mumbo-jumbo.

Emperor Theodosius I outlawed all worship of the Roman deities and closed their temples.

Yet even after this, devotion to the gods lived on, widespread and fairly open, for at least another century. Other changes came, especially following the fall of Rome in 476. Over the centuries, Christianity became more and more firmly entwined with the culture of Europe and, eventually, the Americas. But the names of our months have not changed since Roman times. People have continued to read the stories of Rome's deities in ancient works such as Virgil's *Aeneid* and Ovid's *Metamorphoses*. Images of the goddesses and gods continue to live, too, in countless beautiful paintings and sculptures. Even for people who no longer believe in these deities, there is still much to admire and much that can inspire.

Most inspiring of all, perhaps, is the vision of a world where people of many backgrounds and faiths can look past their differences, see their common humanity, and live together in harmony. This was the vision of Quintus Aurelius Symmachus. In 384 CE, he pleaded with the emperor Valentinian II not to persecute the ancient Roman religion: "We are asking for amnesty for the gods of our fathers, the gods of our homeland." His eloquent defense of religious tolerance continued, in words that echo through the centuries:

> It is reasonable to assume that whatever each of us worships can be considered one and the same. We look up at the same stars, the same sky is above us all, the same universe encompasses us. What difference does it make which system each of us uses to find the truth? It is not by just one route that man can arrive at so great a mystery.

The stories of gods and goddesses continue to shape modern literature and art. We can hope Symmachus's vision of religious tolerance takes hold one day, too.

A painting by Renaissance masters Titian and Bellini depicting a passage from Ovid's *Fasti*

GLOSSARY

atrium

The front room of a Roman house, used to receive visitors.

augur

A Roman priest with the responsibilities of marking out sacred space and of interpreting the will of the gods.

auspices

Signs from the gods, particularly the behavior of birds within an area defined by the augurs.

consecrate

To make holy; to dedicate to religious purposes.

forum

The civic center and main meeting place of a Roman city, with government buildings, offices, shops, and temples surrounding a large open area. In Rome itself, there were six forums: the ancient original Forum, plus additional forums built by Julius Caesar and by the emperors Augustus, Nerva, Vespasian, and Trajan.

inscription

Words written on or carved into lasting materials such as metal and stone.

Latin

The Romans' language, and the official language of the empire. Greek was also widely used, especially in the eastern part of the empire.

matron

A freeborn married woman.

mola salsa

Grain that was roasted, ground, and mixed with salt, used to bless sacrificial animals and as an offering on its own.

orator

A person skilled in making speeches.

pantheon

A term referring to all of the gods and goddesses.

personification

A deity or imaginary being that represents a thing or idea.

pietas

A proper sense of duty and respect.

pontiff

A member of a Roman priesthood concerned mainly with religious law. The Latin word is *pontifex*, and the plural form is *pontifices* (pohn-TI-fi-kays).

province

A territory of the Roman Empire.

relief

A form of sculpture in which the images project out from a flat surface.

rotunda

A very large, round room, typically with a domed roof.

shrine

A small place of worship, usually either outdoors or set aside inside a larger building (such as a wall niche holding a statue of a deity).

Further Information

Books

Adkins, Lesley, and Roy A. Adkins. *Dictionary of Roman Religion.* New York: Facts on File, 1996.

Brandon, S. G. F., and Dean Miller. *Beliefs, Rituals, and Symbols of Ancient Greece and Rome.* New York: Cavendish Square, 2014.

Nardo, Don. *From Founding to Fall: A History of Rome.* San Diego, CA: Lucent Books, 2003.

Websites

Ancient Rome
http://www.history.com/topics/ancient-history/ancient-rome

The History Channel's Ancient Rome page features videos, articles, and even an interactive infographic.

Perseus Collection: Greek and Roman Materials
http://www.perseus.tufts.edu/hopper/collection?collection=Perseus:collection:Greco-Roman

Search Tufts University's online repository for primary-source texts about Roman religion, including writing by Livy, Tacitus, and Cicero.

The Roman Empire in the First Century: Religion
http://www.pbs.org/empires/romans/empire/religion.html

PBS's overview of religion in ancient Rome includes pictures, links, and biographies of key figures.

ORGANIZATIONS

The Classical Association of Canada

http://www.cac-scec.ca

The Classical Association of Canada (CAC) has a wide-reaching mission that includes supporting a classics curriculum in Canadian schools. The CAC's website is a wonderful resource for more information on classics departments at the university level around the country. The organization is also home to two journals.

Society for the Promotion of Roman Studies

http://www.romansociety.org

The Society for the Promotion of Roman Studies was founded in 1910. The organization boasts members from over forty countries and is free to join. The Roman Society, as it's known, also hosts an online image gallery of over four thousand images.

SOURCE NOTES

Chapter 1: The Divine and the Human

p. 7, Turcan, Robert. *The Gods of Ancient Rome: Religion in Everyday Life from Archaic to Imperial Times*. Translated by Antonia Nevill. New York: Routledge, 2000. p. 12

p. 9, Ibid., p. 16

p. 15, Warrior, Valerie M. *Roman Religion*. Cambridge, UK: Cambridge University Press, 2006. p. 50

Chapter 2: Roman Rites

p. 17, Warrior, Valerie M. *Roman Religion*. Cambridge, UK: Cambridge University Press, 2006. p. 2

p. 21, Shelton, Jo-Ann. *As the Romans Did: A Sourcebook in Roman Social History*. 2nd ed. New York: Oxford University Press, 1998. p. 14

p. 21, Warrior, Valerie M. *Roman Religion*. Cambridge, UK: Cambridge University Press, 2006. p. 99

p. 23, Apuleius. *The Golden Ass*. Translated by Jack Lindsay. Bloomington: Indiana University Press, 1962. p. 19

Chapter 3: On Holy Ground

p. 25, Livy. *History of Rome*. Translated by B. O. Foster. Cambridge, MA: Harvard University Press, 1919. p. 5

p. 26, Lewis, C. Day, trans. *The Aeneid of Virgil*. Garden City, NY: Doubleday, 1953. p. 189

p. 27, Vitruvius. *The Ten Books on Architecture*. Translated by Morris Hicky Morgan. New York: Dover Publications, 1960. p. 116

p. 30, Livy. *History of Rome*. Translated by B. O. Foster. Cambridge, MA: Harvard University Press, 1919. p. 13

p. 31, Highet, Gilbert. *Poets in a Landscape.* New York: Alfred A. Knopf, 1957. pp. 89–90

Chapter 4: Spiritual Men

p. 33, Warrior, Valerie M. *Roman Religion.* Cambridge, UK: Cambridge University Press, 2006. p. 59

p. 35, Turcan, Robert. *The Gods of Ancient Rome: Religion in Everyday Life from Archaic to Imperial Times.* Translated by Antonia Nevill. New York: Routledge, 2000. p. 17

p. 36, Beard, Mary, et al. *Religions of Rome. Volume I: A History.* Cambridge, UK: Cambridge University Press, 1998. p. 115

p. 37, Shelton, Jo-Ann. *As the Romans Did: A Sourcebook in Roman Social History.* 2nd ed. New York: Oxford University Press, 1998. p. 384

p. 37, Ibid., p. 385

Chapter 5: Religious Women

p. 41, Cicero. "M. Tullius Cicero, *For Marcus Fonteius.*" Perseus Digital Library. Retrieved June 13, 2016. http://www.perseus.tufts.edu/hopper/text?doc=Perseus:text:1999.02.0019:text.

p. 42, Shelton, Jo-Ann. *As the Romans Did: A Sourcebook in Roman Social History.* 2nd ed. New York: Oxford University Press, 1998. p. 386

p. 43, Fantham, Elaine, et al. *Women in the Classical World: Image and Text.* New York: Oxford University Press, 1994. p. 362

p. 46, Apuleius. *The Golden Ass.* Translated by Jack Lindsay. Bloomington: Indiana University Press, 1962. pp. 240–241

pp. 46–47, Tacitus, Cornelius. *Annals and Histories.* Translated by A. J. Church and William Jackson Brodribb. Translated by Eleanor Cowan. London: Everyman, 2009. pp. 186–187

Chapter 6: Marking Life's Transitions

p. 49, Warrior, Valerie M. *Roman Religion.* Cambridge, UK: Cambridge University Press, 2006. p. 38

p. 52, MacMullen, Ramsay, and Eugene N. Lane. *Paganism and Christianity 100–425 CE: A Sourcebook*. Minneapolis: Fortress Press, 1992. p. 107

p. 52, Shelton, Jo-Ann. *As the Romans Did: A Sourcebook in Roman Social History.* 2nd ed. New York: Oxford University Press, 1998. p. 430

p. 53, Warrior, Valerie M. *Roman Religion*. Cambridge, UK: Cambridge University Press, 2006. p. 40

p. 53, Virgil. *The Aeneid.* Translated by Robert Fagles. New York: Penguin Books, 2006. p. 177

Chapter 7: Holidays and Festivals

p. 55, Ovid, Peter Wiseman, and Anne Wiseman. *Fasti*. Oxford, UK: Oxford University Press, 2013. p. 9

p. 59, Ibid., p. 26

p. 60, Turcan, Robert. *The Gods of Ancient Rome: Religion in Everyday Life from Archaic to Imperial Times.* Translated by Antonia Nevill. New York: Routledge, 2000. p. 35

Chapter 8: Harmony and Discord

p. 63, Warrior, Valerie M. *Roman Religion*. Cambridge, UK: Cambridge University Press, 2006. p. 16

pp. 64–65, *The Holy Bible*, Revised Standard Version, Mark 12:17.

p. 66, Shelton, Jo-Ann. *As the Romans Did: A Sourcebook in Roman Social History.* 2nd ed. New York: Oxford University Press, 1998. p. 405

p. 67, Warrior, Valerie M. *Roman Religion*. Cambridge, UK: Cambridge University Press, 2006. p. 80

p. 68, Shelton, Jo-Ann. *As the Romans Did: A Sourcebook in Roman Social History.* 2nd ed. New York: Oxford University Press, 1998. p. 405

BIBLIOGRAPHY

Adkins, Lesley, and Roy A. Adkins. *Dictionary of Roman Religion.* New York: Facts on File, 1996.

———. *Handbook to Life in Ancient Rome.* New York: Oxford University Press, 1994.

Apuleius. *The Golden Ass.* Translated by Jack Lindsay. Bloomington: Indiana University Press, 1962.

Beard, Mary, et al. *Religions of Rome. Volume I: A History.* Cambridge, UK: Cambridge University Press, 1998.

Cicero. "M. Tullius Cicero, *For Marcus Fonteius.*" Perseus Digital Library. Retrieved June 13, 2016. http://www.perseus.tufts.edu/hopper/text?doc=Perseus:text:1999.02.0019:text.

Fantham, Elaine, et al. *Women in the Classical World: Image and Text.* New York: Oxford University Press, 1994.

Hallett, Judith P. "Women in the Ancient Roman World." In *Women's Roles in Ancient Civilizations: A Reference Guide*, edited by Bella Vivante, 257–289. Westport, CT: Greenwood Press, 1999.

Highet, Gilbert. *Poets in a Landscape.* New York: Alfred A. Knopf, 1957.

Kraemer, Ross Shepard. *Her Share of the Blessings: Women's Religions Among Pagans, Jews, and Christians in the Greco-Roman World.* New York: Oxford University Press, 1992.

Lewis, C. Day, trans. *The Aeneid of Virgil.* Garden City, NY: Doubleday, 1953.

Lewis, Naphtali, and Meyer Reinhold, eds. *Roman Civilization, Sourcebook II: The Empire.* New York: Harper & Row, 1966.

Livy. *History of Rome.* Translated by B. O. Foster. Cambridge, MA: Harvard University Press, 1919.

MacMullen, Ramsay, and Eugene N. Lane. *Paganism and Christianity 100–425 CE: A Sourcebook*. Minneapolis: Fortress Press, 1992.

Meyer, Marvin W., ed. *The Ancient Mysteries: A Sourcebook*. San Francisco: Harper & Row, 1987.

Ovid, Peter Wiseman, and Anne Wiseman. *Fasti*. Oxford: Oxford University Press, 2013.

Shelton, Jo-Ann. *As the Romans Did: A Sourcebook in Roman Social History*. 2nd ed. New York: Oxford University Press, 1998.

Tacitus, Cornelius. *Annals and Histories*. Translated by A. J. Church and William Jackson Brodribb. Translated by Eleanor Cowan. London: Everyman, 2009.

Turcan, Robert. *The Gods of Ancient Rome: Religion in Everyday Life from Archaic to Imperial Times*. Translated by Antonia Nevill. New York: Routledge, 2000.

Virgil. *The Aeneid*. Translated by Robert Fagles. New York: Penguin Books, 2006.

Vitruvius. *The Ten Books on Architecture*. Translated by Morris Hicky Morgan. New York: Dover Publications, 1960.

Warrior, Valerie M. *Roman Religion*. Cambridge, UK: Cambridge University Press, 2006.

Wells, Colin. *The Roman Empire*. 2nd ed. Cambridge, MA: Harvard University Press, 1992.

INDEX

Page numbers in **boldface** are illustrations. Entries in **boldface** are glossary terms.